AMARANTH

Robert Carr

Bob - Thank you for joining me at The Mount.

AMARANTH

Robert Carr

Indolent Books

Book design: kd diamond
Cover art: WT McRae

Published by Indolent Books,
an imprint of Indolent Enterprises, LLC

www.indolentbooks.com
Brooklyn, New York

ISBN: 978-1-945023-02-6

CONTENTS

Prince's Feather

Equinox...11

Two..12

Merman..13

Clay..14

Sleeping Apart..15

The Flower Show..16

Porch in a Storm..17

Closing the Grand View..18

Magnolias...19

Goosefoot

G.R.I.D. 23

Valentine..24

Black Dog of Vieques...25

Gristle..26

Apothecary...27

Hawk..28

Bedside...29

Cage...30

Milk Bath...31

Wormseed

Cremation..35

Acadia..36

Anniversary..37

Removing the Poet's Desk..38

Before You..39

Unseen...40

The Holiday Poem..41

Shirts...42

Speaking in Flowers...43

For my husband, Stephen Rivais

The spirit culls
Unfaded amaranth, when wild it strays
Through the old garden—ground of boyish days.

— *John Keats*

Prince's Feather

Equinox

I dream you
in your grass stained towel

on your grass stained knees
I am your turned field row

your fresh fingered
crewcut hill

your back flattened hay
at the edge of a wood

set your thumb
between my lips

reset your baseball cap
cast shadow

protect
your reddened neck

I pray you
come with spring

in you
my arm-pinned funk

stampede
an open heat filled barn

Two

We rarely talk, except through blue jeaned
knees beneath a diner counter.
On Saturdays at Wash and Fold we drop
the family clothes, then drive in separate cars

to the motel room on 202. We stand
between the yellow spreads of noon twin beds.
Greasy headboards bare brass screwed
into a wall where the prints of strangers shine.

The fisheye lens of a metal door is peephole empty
sunlit view. The parking lot breaks in the jalousie
windows above a beige-chipped air conditioner whine.
A noise to drown the moans of Pay Per View.

Cracks in mirror split merry-go-round
motion as cool hands hold your hips.
One more spin to fill our mouths
with another tongue.

You pull up pants. Rings and keys
drop in a telltale pocket. I clip ID to my belt,
glance back toward two beds—one tightly tucked,
the other a pot of sheets boiled over.

Merman

I step barefoot
around broken asphalt

at the launch, finding
half the severed

body of a pike.
Lake water floats

the white pearl
of his long belly.

I wonder where
the half-man torso

has been tossed—
the young merman lost,

the gray-pink
of trim waist discarded

among sharp green
blades of cattails.

Clay

The child curls in a grassy flannel field
of mounted cowboys and cattle brands.
He fingers the flat white buttons
along the edge of his pajamas.
His mother reads his favorite, gentle Ferdinand
the bull, cork tree shaded before the sting.

She wears her black fur coat, her hair is fancy.
His small hands burrow in the perfumed pelt.
Clay is right downstairs. Sleep tight!
She kisses the palm of his hand and closes
the door. He hears Clay laughing and the TV show.
His darkened eyes, his sleepy lashes loll and start.

An inverted L of light appears and disappears.
The door silently opens and closes.
The flashlight's green eye approaches,
he can't see the blue-veined hand that holds it.
Playing possum—his darting eyes open just a crack
as three-ringed light scans the rodeo of his pajamas—

Clay rolls the boy onto his back.
The flashlight, resting on the bedside stand
makes magical rings on the ceiling, exposes
hairline cracks in plaster. In the outer oval,
where the curtains hang still and heavy
on their rod, the boy imagines Charlotte
in her web and goes to sit beside her.

Sleeping Apart

We were counseled
to sleep in the same room
but knew a nightly
absence would be missed.

Sleeping apart we practice
listening through walls,
wrap ourselves in sheets
of different shade,

turn toward whom
we hope to find.
Undisturbed, we reach
open fingered into a tingle

to touch unlit air—
thrash and throw bedside
lamps to the floor,
dream our daylight sex

in other rooms—on the dining
table cleared of candlelight—
in the attic, holding the chipped
red paint of stairs.

The Flower Show

Mama melts away beneath the shoulders
of her butter yellow suit. We hold tight to arms,
to the handles of a borrowed chair. Winter
cheekboned eyes cast the red-rimmed
pouch of orchids as we wheel the flower show.

The air is earth, a forced bulb backlit landscape,
a rubber black walkway. Out of order—hyacinth
spikes beside delphinium, dogwood pops summer
buttons over confused crocus. No one would guess—

Koi turn slowly in their lotus pool, chair spokes
catch the crease of her yellow jacket—ruined. Manikins
wear crowns of sunlit replica, water streams
over the drilled skull of a fountain globe. Smiling,
she asks if I remember bathing in her sink.

Porch in a Storm

Naked behind the storm
bang of his screened door,
I watch for a red truck.

His call on the cell, a mist
of spit through screen on skin.
Be ready babe.

I stand waiting
with hardened gut,
nipple-tight balls.

The mud door slams—
a ripped screen sound
on broken branch

as a knot in my throat loosens—
blood-lipped, standing flame,
fast wood with tearing eyes

we burn in a forest of distant
beating hands. Collapsed
in our sorries, on the floor

beneath his weight, I understand
why he cries and licks
my familiar salt.

Closing The Grand View

Just outside China
on the way to Belfast,
Bette served breakfast
for a good many years
at the Grand View Topless Grill.

On Saturdays she smoothed
her skirt of patriotic denim
with hands that rubbed Intensive Care
over breasts and arms before a shift.

Pete loved his wife
and Bette's brown nipples
as she leaned to pour his coffee
or used her terry towel
to buff the red Formica.

The sun through diner blinds
striped Pete's home fry steam
the day he heard—
the Grand View was closing.

It's a tear-down, for a self-storage,
Bette confided. *That's a shame,*
Pete agreed, as his hand trembled
holding the ironstone mug.

Magnolias

The white meat of magnolia blossom
was long on the hook since spring
insisted an unusual cool.

Then, a sun scorched crow
landed in branches
and clutched the pink parrots.

Almost to a bird, they fell to earth
and died of fear. Blush gray wings
silent, folded on a walkway.

Some fell fresh, roseate
children on a pyre. Others
gasped, the brown inhale of lung.

A walk through fallen flowers
leaves foot-sign rot. Treads of boot
stamp—a lifeless burst of feather.

Goosefoot

G.R.I.D.

Come into me unsheathed
strand, little death hood
between boy and man.

Simmer in the warm lining
of my ass. Dance as I play
percussion on the empty
case of your clarinet,

the beat that burns
the blond of loved arms
to nub, the singeing stink
of your match.

Come over me, decade
of brownouts as I plunge
fingers into a rib cage
and split myself to you.

Come around me, clustering
of little boy smells, raging stain
dripping absence of color
from a bag on a pole.

Come, come to me
in the startled brow
of a lover who called me
his only one,

the small voice saying
the sarcoma on his arm
is a birthmark I've forgotten.

Valentine

You gave me white tulips in clear water
I gave you flesh shaped crystal

You gave me fringed white parrots
I gave you our son's hazel corn silk view

White tulips—along one binding petal
we cross a red line

a small streak of mosquito
on our white wall

Black Dog of Vieques

Though her whiskered snout
has grayed

and a hairless tumor
rises on her hippy rump

and her young brown friend
watching from the grassy roadside

has lost his leg—
she will force your brake

look through you
with her yellow

pus-teared eye
dismiss your slack stare

as she nuzzles
dead iguana and lopes away

cold-blooded meal
dangling from her mouth

thanking the lizard
with her wagging tail

Gristle

The soldier secretly eats
the skin from his peeling

feet. A meager taste,
the texture—used wax paper—

seems rich, like lamb
gristle. His front tooth nibble

is a sharp tremor. It helps
him remember that before—

a kitchen, it was yellow as it burned,
there was a woman and she broiled.

Apothecary

The bone of phone speak rattles
at my hip—a New Orleans vial
sent by conjurer, magic in cobalt

corked on a soot skinned
shelf. His pictures sync
in many names—Amaranth:

a raised chin of prince's feather,
my goosefoot curl of toes,
his sweet of wormseed.

The screen—a millipede
loads a slow and circling rune.
I stroke his image

with a thumb to open
his virtual mouth. My need—
his threaded worm needle,

the lash of his whip
dark skin, his sex spell
hooked and healed. Pendulous,

undying flower—I wet
my finger to pale blue knuckle
dip in rare unbottled powder.

Hawk

A blood-traced
feather bib
blends on a branch
of snow bent
hemlock
below the golden
butcher
of his hook.
He is pure yank
sabre eyed.
Young raccoon
sprawled across
his January perch—
the hawk cocky
as a bar stool drunk
with a bowie.

Bedside

When I ask
what you need
you say Death,

but the steady
spoon you hold
in the bowl,

the hand
and the arm,
thin as space

in my meditation
of thumb
and forefinger,

says, *No.*
The oxygen
whispers

beside your bed—
Just wait... Just wait...
Just wait...

You sleep,
a hollow hand
on mine, until

your one eye opens—
You're so handsome.

The squeeze, a close
clipped yellow nail.

Cage

Did your brown eye
look for my brown eye
as your life
your unchecked
watery shit ran out?
Did you wonder
where I was?
Did your thumb slide
the mortared groove
of a cinder block wall
remembering
through thick paint
the living line of my jaw?
Did your breath break
as mine does now
knowing you were wet
alone and caged—
not in my arms, not under
my whispering hand
counting your ribs,
slowing your heart?

Milk Bath

When you died last night
the relief escaped location.

Your sister's cautious call
reached around to scratch my back,

the fork that tested evening cornbread
came out clean.

Behind the desk drawer pull,
behind the balled rubber bands,

under the collars left behind
without a dog, I find our rings.

Relieved I'm not there to see your body,
I run a scalding water in the tub.

The velvet ring box is open on the sink,
bath salts turn a steam to milk.

Once again, a slippery knuckle refuses
your band as I lower myself into a burn.

Wormseed

Cremation

In a still parking lot
my father grips the wheel
as if driving very fast.

Her powdered smell,
her box of tissues
unopened on the dash.

Did daubed lips
leave a keepsake shade
in the pocket of her door?

He counts steps, looks ahead—
Simple, Affordable, Dignified
stenciled on the door.

He pauses before entering
the iced box air
where someone hovers.

He imagines
he should speak—
For pick up?

Someone pushes a button
on a counter—*Carr for Mary Lou.*
Somewhere, a speaker—

About ten minutes, we're scraping her out.
A light, a hum, someone is falling.
He can smell her powder.

Acadia

On the lichen freckled slab
of a great rock in Acadia

I think—
not much happens here.

Words come at me
like handfuls of low bush blueberries

that miss an open mouth.
I sit between my stanzas

and a stack of piled flat stones.
I skim, one by one

toward my reflection
in the bowl of a far off lake.

Anniversary

When you released my hand
your palm opened like a dry sponge
suddenly soaked and swollen.
I took the unsipped glass beside our bed
and poured the water carefully
into the blue chambers of an ice tray.

I stored the hardened cubes
in the white washcloth
I used to soothe your sores.
I filled your running sock
with the amber row of bottles
that repeat your name.

Unused oval tablets to ease your pain
rolled slow seasons, hidden in our drawer.
You said, *Wait a year, it'll get better—*

Tonight I've kept my promise.
I marked the day on your calendar
inside the cellar door.
You wouldn't like this wet ring
as year old melting ice sweats glass
staining our nightstand.

As I close my hand, lying cool
as winter sheets, you watch me
from the picture of you swimming.
Beside the childproof caps
I breathe relieved the absent
bleach of your empty sock.

Removing The Poet's Desk

The walled hollow space
　　　echoes my stepping.

A dusty edge of drawer
　　　defines your mark.

A single almond
　　　you left on the floor

says more
　　　than all your words.

Calloused nut
　　　balanced on my fingertip—

Unsown, I consider
　　　dropping the seed.

Before You

there was a youth
he jerked off
his joy in the mirror
he jerked off
brushing teeth
under a pilled robe
in the spine
of open books
on the fantasy—
Jonny Quest
on Hadji
in the cowboy hat
of the Rifleman
he didn't know
before death
he didn't know
that you
would show up
take the toothbrush
take the robe
the books
rip off the story
crack the screen
he didn't know
that you were out
there waiting

Unseen

He probes her glossy mouth as if to reach
inside and lick from throat to bottom.

The heat between them hides me
as she settles on the wall.

Her thumbs slide dark lace
to her ankles.

I see his shadowed face
beneath her skirt's flounced shell.

I taste the scuffed
heel-up sole of sandy shoes

as touring cars circle
the roundabout.

That night his tongue
tickles new formed toes

a father's smooth lapping
at the wisps of my soft crown.

The Holiday Poem

I read my poetry at the holiday table
but this year was told explicitly, *Don't.*
This year, Dad brought his own poem
by his favorite author, Mary Oliver.

So my father convenes my court
and opens *Blue Horses*. He reads
about yoga, being unable
to touch toes as Mary turns
into a lotus.

My sister breathes
for the first time in ten years,
This is the best Christmas ever!

It seems not everyone
enjoys tears at the table
or the blood of dead mothers
in their cranberry sauce.

I decide to forgive myself:
Let the soft animal of my body
love what it loves
and curl up on the couch.

Shirts

1.
The unlinked cuffs of my father's
starched white sleeves roll
up boy-thin sunburned arms.
I skip along and drag his tails behind,
sanding his shirt in shore foam
shimmer, Ocean City flecks of mica.

2.
Our smell is tee shirt need and sweat—
a tuxedoed boy rips pearled stud buttons
from the stiff placket of my shirt.
Black silk bow tie, undone around my neck—
I squeeze the wiry ginger of his crotch as he floats
kisses in the dip behind my collarbone.

3.
The rain spits my shirt to bare pink skin.
Beads of water tremble our favorite flowers.
I run a graveyard lawn as cold mist rises
from the grass and through my veins.
I tear the proper cotton from my chest,
press my solitary body to mossed stone.

4.
Tomorrow, I will button a white shirt.
It will hang on bone, slope with shoulder,
hold its form. I will not roll French cuffs
to my bicep, or dance with shirttails through sand,
or sniff for kisses beneath my collar, or run
in rain, or scout a shirtless figure in the haze.

Speaking in Flowers

Tonight we'll share a breath
of pollen, exhale toward the lunar

language of this September.
We'll whisper through

the passing clouds
as they stretch a pink vein

between us. Starting today—
we speak in the windpipe

weight of amaranth,
in the barbed legs

of bees on day lilies,
in the red checkerberry

carpet of beads at the twiggy
root of mountain laurel.

ACKNOWLEDGMENTS

These poems originally appeared, sometimes in different versions, in the following publications.

4ink7: "The Holiday Poem"
Bewildering Stories Magazine: "Gristle"
Canary Literary Journal: "Hawk"
Eunoia Literary Review: "Shirts"
Front Porch Literary Review: "Acadia," "Moving the Poet's Desk"
Good Men Project: "Sleeping Apart"
HIV Here and Now: "Before You"
Pickled Body Poetry and Arts Magazine: "Two"
White Stag Literary Journal: "Black Dog," "Merman," "Works"

My return to poetry would not have happened without the guidance of many people, but particularly my husband of 27 years, Stephen, and our son Noah. You are my greatest teachers in that most simple and complicated of lessons—love. Passionate thanks to my father, my sister, and my chosen family—you know who you are. Many thanks to my teachers and mentors: Mark Halliday, Ada Limon, and Tom Daley. Thanks to those who read individual poems and drafts of this book including Cammy Thomas, Dorian Kotsiopolis and all of the wonderful poets I've met and worked with in writing workshops in Boston and Provincetown. Gratitude to my dear friend Ken Jones Jr. who designed the poetry website robertcarr.org; to the editors of *Amaranth*, April Ossman and Tom Daley; and to Michael H. Broder and his vision for Indolent Books.

ABOUT THE AUTHOR

Robert Carr was born in Annapolis, Maryland and grew up in New Hampshire. He holds a BA in Philosophy from Bates College in Lewiston, Maine and a MEd in counseling psychology from the University of Massachusetts. He is Deputy Director, Bureau of Infectious Disease and Laboratory Sciences at the Massachusetts Department of Public Health. *Amaranth* is his first collection.

ABOUT INDOLENT BOOKS

Indolent Books is a small independent press founded in 2015 and operating in Brooklyn. Indolent was founded as a home for poets of a certain age who have done the creative work but for whatever reason (family, career, self—effacement, etc.) have not published a first collection. But we are not dogmatic about that mission: Ultimately, we publish books we like and care about, short or long, poetry or prose. We are queer owned, queer staffed, and maintain a commitment to diversity among our authors, artists, designers, developers, and other team members.

CPSIA information can be obtained
at www.ICGtesting.com
Printed in the USA
BVOW03s2351221116

468663BV00001B/32/P